WRITERS AND THEIR W

ISOBEL ARMSTRONG
General Editor

BRYAN LOUGHREY
Advisory Editor

George Herbert

GEORGE HERBERT

after an engraving by R. WHITE *which first appeared in Izaac Walton's*
'Life', 1670 and in the 1674 edition of 'THE TEMPLE'

George Herbert

T. S. Eliot

Introduction by Peter Porter

Northcote House

in association with
The British Council

© Copyright 1962 by T. S. Eliot
Introduction © Copyright 1994 by Peter Porter

This edition, with new introduction and bibliography, first published in 1994 by
Northcote House Publishers Ltd, Plymbridge House, Estover Road,
Plymouth PL6 7PZ, United Kingdom. Tel: (0752) 735251. Fax: (0752) 695699.

British Library Cataloguing-in-Publication Data
A catalogue record for this book is available from the British Library

ISBN 0 7463 0746 2

Typeset by PDQ Typesetting, Stoke-on-Trent
Printed and bound in the United Kingdom by BPC Wheatons Ltd, Exeter

Contents

Biographical Outline   vi

Note on the Text   vii

Introduction   PETER PORTER   1

George Herbert   T. S. ELIOT   11

1   Life and Background   13

2   *The Temple*   22

3   Herbert and Donne   32

4   Notes   40

Select Bibliography   41

Index   47

Biographical Outline

1593	Born at Montgomery Castle, 3 April.
1596	Father, Sir Richard Herbert, dies.
1605	Sent to Westminster School and subsequently awarded a scholarship to Trinity College, Cambridge.
1615	Elected a Fellow of Trinity College, Cambridge.
1619	Made Public Orator to the University.
1624–5	Elected MP for Montgomery.
1626	Becomes a deacon in the Church of England.
1627	His mother, Lady Magdalen Herbert of Montgomery, dies.
	Resigns his oratorship.
1629	Marries Jane Danvers.
1630	Becomes an ordained priest and obtains the living of Bemerton in Wiltshire where he serves as a conscientious and benevolent rector until his death.
1633	Sends a collection of verse to his friend Nicholas Ferrar for his opinion.
	Dies on 3 March and is buried in Bemerton.
	Following Herbert's death Ferrar publishes the collection of verse *The Temple*. By 1680 *The Temple* has gone through 13 editions.

Note on the Text

T. S. Eliot and Peter Porter have quoted from different editions of George Herbert's works as a result of which minor differences in the presentation of some of the poems occur.

The edition used by Peter Porter is *George Herbert: The Complete English Poems*, edited by John Tobin (London: Penguin 1991).

Introduction

Peter Porter

We are accustomed to assume that writers' reputations will change every century or so, even to the extent that the Pantheon itself may, like some refurbished museum, or Madame Tussaud's, face a crisis and choose to clear out some famous figures and install others not previously thought worth exhibiting. We further conclude that the taste of our time is not simply a natural consequence of how we see past literature but that our vision is scientifically accurate, that indeed our valuation is how things truly are, and all opinion-making before ours was either a preparation for our full judgement or a mistaken assessment in need of our redress. Some artists (I include painters as well as writers since the history of painting presents a clearer outline than does that of literature) have never been questioned as centrally important masters – Titian, Rubens and Watteau, or Shakespeare, Milton and Pope. Others, though, have suffered eclipse after their deaths and then, sometimes centuries later, been restored to the very highest plinth of the Pantheon – Piero della Francesca and John Donne are an effective pairing here. Still others, though never forgotten, have seen their place in the tradition fluctuate like equities on the Stock Exchange. Marvells have continued to rise this century, Blakes are rather flat and Matthew Arnolds have sunk: Raphaels, once the top quotation of all, have lost value seriously, only to come back strongly.

These examples, drawn from the City and from fashion writing, are not as frivolous as they seem. One aspect of the serious study of literature which is seldom acknowledged is the enormous bulk of past achievement which competes for the attention of readers and scholars. Like a note played on a violin which will also sound sympathetic notes which are its harmonics, past writings may appeal over the heads of their immediate inheritors to a present-day sensibility. It doesn't matter too much if the presumption of

1

the modern reader includes misunderstandings of the historical background of the author. It is in this sense that the notion that all art is contemporary may be usefully understood. The revolutionary impact of the Donne revival at the beginning of the twentieth century is an obvious example of the chiming of sensibilities across the years. Today the Metaphysical Poets are probably better known than the Romantics. Literary valuation is never static: greatness can be forgotten as well as perceived; enlisted or misappropriated; revalued up or down; and is constantly being defined for our own purposes.

Of all 'the school of Donne', George Herbert is the poet who has come most sharply into our consciousness at this millennial date – more so even that the master himself. His eclipse was as total as that of Donne: only Isaac Walton's *Life* kept his reputation intact for two centuries after his death and that in itself is an indicator of the way his reputation was to go once the Herbert revival started – namely as an adornment of Anglicanism. Piety rather than poetry was in the minds of his esteemers until recently. One particularly unfortunate result of this was the strange spectacle of a virtuoso being loved for qualities the very opposite of bravura, for a sort of mousy Anglican honesty. That Herbert is perhaps the most honest poet who ever wrote in English does not prevent his being also one of the most accomplished technicians of verse in the whole canon. One critic who saw this, as T. S. Eliot points out, was Coleridge, always an original judge of poetry, who recognized that Herbert's playfulness was profound and not quaint.

Eliot, who by the time he wrote his British Council study in 1962 had mellowed from the severity of *For Lancelot Andrewes* and *Thoughts After Lambeth*, emphasizes the Anglicanism but presents it in its less polemical guise. Earlier, he would probably have stressed Herbert's doctrinal toughness, a combativeness which was natural to his age and which he shares with Donne. Becoming a parish priest instead of a court apologist did turn Herbert's poetry towards ordinary human concerns and fitted out his metaphorical style with an unrivalled array of down-to-earth properties, but Herbert conceded not an inch to plainness: his conceits and devices continue unassuaged through his didactic performance. Eliot justly deprecates the village green aspect of Anglicanism which for so long Herbert lovers foisted on us, but he does not go as far as W. H. Auden in his brief introduction to a Penguin Selection made in 1973. In discussing the poem 'The British Church', Auden directs our attention to Herbert's sense of the aesthetic rightness of Anglicanism – its liturgy, its use of images and music, and its just balance of enthusiasm and decorum. The Thirty-Nine Articles are not neglected, but the use to which theology is put is a matter for each believer. Between 'The British Church' and later Anglican polemics such as Bishop Burnet's homily on the death of the Earl of Rochester a great gap yawns. Anglicanism becomes more vehement and evangelical. It loses intellectual rigour to pick up sentimental persuasiveness. It is hooked on death-bed repentance and self-accusation. Reading Herbert's poems takes us back to the perihelion of the Church of England. Herbert wrote only religious verse: he was always the pastor, the vicar of his flock and by extension of the world beyond the church porch, but he lived in the open – his poetry is in the best sense committed to the mundane as well as the celestial.

Auden, also writing at the end of a long career as communicator and poet, makes the up-to-date observation that Herbert is one of the very few artists of genius he'd have liked to know personally. Auden seems to believe that the truthfulness and compassion as well as the wit and technical address of Herbert's verse would guarantee his being an agreeable companion. I suppose that compared to the hauteur of Dante, the vanity of Pope and the squalor of Rimbaud, Herbert is a healthy and natural presence. However, poets are usually not much like their poetry, and Eliot's emphasis on Herbert's pride of lineage, his consciousness of being above his parishioners in birth and education, modified though it was by faith, is closer to the real position. What Auden's pleasantry does point to is nevertheless important: Herbert is one of us, if 'us' be taken to represent the temperament of the late twentieth century. Poets and readers of poetry alike feel at home with Herbert. I cannot think of another poet in the long march of English Verse who speaks to us so clearly and with such authority as Herbert does. And this sense of communication is achieved at a time when orthodox Christianity is at its lowest ebb. We have all heeded the warning not to read the Bible for its prose, so our love of Herbert is not an esteeming of art over faith. Rather it seems to be our wonderment at the perfect matching of technique to utterance, the discovery of a natural voice which, while never cracking into falsehood or swelling to pomposity, attains the very height of eloquence. The practising poet examining a Herbert poem is like someone bending over a Rolls-Royce engine. How is it all done? Why can't I make something so elaborate and yet so simple? Why is a machine which performs so well also so beautiful? One approach to Herbert's poetry is suggested by both Eliot and Auden. He got much of his intellectual machinery from Donne, his mother's admired friend and encomiast. But he was able to add something which Donne lacked – a sense of music. He was an accomplished and assured musician. While Donne's poems, for all their grandeur, are assembled like Meccano or Lego, structures bolted together, Herbert's are more like musical compositions, extensions of themes whose spans are both lyrical and precisely placed. Many critics have remarked on the appearance of his poems on the page, but too much concentration on imitative shapes of the more downright sort, such as 'Easter Wings', rather misses the point. A Herbert stanza is not some anticipation of Concrete Poetry; instead it is, like sonata form, variation technique or passacaglia, a way of developing a theme through many divagations. Every poet discovers pretty soon when he comes to compose poetry that having something to say is not enough. What is needed is a trellis to train his eloquence on. Contrivance, however, must never be at the expense of naturalness. Herbert shows that proper proportioning, though a tall order, can be done, though we may not fully understand how. (It is a nice fancy to imagine a lost Herbert poem called 'The Trellis'.)

Herbert's remarkable accommodation of musicality to meaning can be seen in 'Prayer I', one of his poems which has always been admired and which T. S. Eliot discusses. Like Shakespeare's Sonnet 66, it is a list, that well-tried option in verse ever since Homer described the fleet setting out for Troy. Both Shakespeare's and Herbert's lists are metaphorical ones but Herbert is much more virtuosic. (He employs the same three quatrain and a couplet form of the sonnet as Shakespeare, though he rhymes differently within the quatrain.) This is the metaphysical mode at full strength, but notice how beautiful the poem is simply as sound. The forensic twists which Empson called 'argufying', the oxymorons, the concertina'd images, the metaphorical audacities which might be described as 'Martianism avant la lettre' – all these effects are subsidiary to the baroque music of the versifying.

Prayer the Church's banquet, Angels age,
   God's breath in man returning to his birth,
   The soul in paraphrase, heart in pilgrimage,
   The Christian plummet sounding heaven and earth;
Engine against the' Almighty, sinners' tower,
   Reversed thunder, Christ-side-piercing spear,
   The six days world transposing in an hour,
A kind of tune, which all things hear and fear;
Softness, and peace, and joy, and love, and bliss,
   Exalted manna, gladness of the best,
   Heaven in ordinary, man well dressed,
The milky way, the bird of Paradise,
   Church-bells beyond the stars heard, the soul's blood,
   The land of spices; something understood.

The whole poem is exquisitely scored. The second part of the last line is a sudden pianissimo after a crescendo; the phrasing is subtly varied throughout and the compositional technique musicians call 'sequence' is applied with due regard to natural succession. The comparison with Shakespeare can be extended to one with Herbert's mentor, Donne. Donne could be musical and intellectual at once – for example in his Holy Sonnet 'Since she whom I loved ...'. Putting 'Prayer' up against another of the Holy Sonnets, 'Batter my heart ...', the poem Eliot chose for direct comparison with it, shows what very different poets Herbert and Donne are. It is usually said that while Donne tortures himself into belief, Herbert is the born embodiment of serenity and grace. However, the difference might be more helpfully described as music (Herbert) and rhetoric (Donne). The beauty of 'Prayer' does not detract from its Christian seriousness. There is a world of doctrine packed into so short a span of poetry. The startling metaphors, 'The Christian plummet sounding heaven and earth', 'God's breath in man returning to his birth', 'Church-bells beyond the stars heard' are not simply poetic fancies but are nuclei of dogma which expand in the mind to illustrate essentials of Christian understanding and belief. In this kind of metaphysical poetry stylistics and subject matter go hand in hand. The ludic method of Herbert and Donne does not permit us to challenge their sincerity. It's true that Herbert himself in the first of his poems entitled 'Jordan' puts his own practice to the test – 'Is all good structure in a winding stair?', and 'Shepherds are honest people; let them sing'. Where would a sophisticated poet look when examining the relation of truth to elegance if not among the products of his own strong propensity? Herbert would surely assent to Touchstone's credo, explaining poetry to yokels in *As You Like It*: 'The truest poetry is the most feigning'. Between these two sentences – Herbert's questioning of his 'winding stair', and Shakespeare's testing of straightforwardness by what is 'most feigning' – the whole of poetry lies. In poem after poem by Herbert we begin by admiring the abruptness, go on to wonder at the singularity of the argument, sometimes even its bizarreness, but end up being awed by the moral rightness of what is said. We see why invention matters, why cleverness is not the enemy of seriousness. What else could have kept Herbert's poetry so fresh? Matthew Arnold's 'melancholy long withdrawing roar' of the sea of faith is no match for the ageless freshness of Herbert's epiphanic sound.

Herbert was unquestionably serious when he composed the poems which make up *The Temple*. This was as conscious a practical service to his God as the three cycles of cantatas were which J. S. Bach wrote for the Lutheran Church in Leipzig covering the Sundays and festal days of the ecclesiastic calendar. But evoking this further musical equivalent reveals immediately the difference between an art which lives by performance and one which brings its benefits only through absorption and study. Walton stresses that Herbert took his pastoral duties seriously and worried that his congregation understood the sacraments and teaching of the Anglican Church. But he would not have distributed his poems among his rural congregation. He might not have concerned himself even with a readership of any sort, though the poems obviously circulated among admirers, as Donne's did. Their survival after his early death shows that there was a circle which valued them, as does his dispatching *The Temple* to his friend Nicholas Ferrar before his demise, however. The mystery remains that such superbly persuasive poetry should nevertheless be confined to the study. But this is the manner of baroque in England. While in Italy baroque took the form of Bernini's carvings and architectural extravagance, in England it was almost purely literary and strangely private, largely a wrestling of worldly consciences with God. At first sight, Herbert's direct addressing of God, for all its couching itself in the language of penitence, seems Un-Anglican, verging on

Puritan familiarity. But, as Donne's poems, not least the Holy Sonnets, also show, this is the nature of metaphysical poetry. The public and outward manner, with all its rhetoric and tendency to elaborate rituals of confession, is conducted inside the form of art; meditation becomes as haunted and dramatic as any temptation experienced by St Anthony in the desert. Of course Herbert is more certain of God's goodness than Donne could ever bring himself to be. Donne's greatest religious poems are products of his restless interregnum at Mitcham, before he took holy orders. Once a clergyman, he abandoned verse in favour of the more extravagant devices of the prose sermon. Herbert's poetry is not only confined to religious subjects, it mostly dates from his later years as an Anglican parson.

Herbert's serenity should not be taken for granted. In certain moods he can be as serious a wrangler as Pascal. Like Pascal, though, he always pursues a lightness of structure and argument, a sort of mathematical balance which makes his poetry the most graceful of any in English. In 'The Answer', we find him deploying a sense of sin theatrically, living and dying in the 'dark state of tears'.

> My comforts drop and fall away like snow:
> I shake my head, and all the thoughts and ends,
> Which my fierce youth did bandy, fall and flow
> Like leaves about me: or like summer friends,
> Flies of estates and sunshine.

But at the sonnet's end, the rabbit is out of the hat:

> to all, that so
> Show me, and set me, I have one reply,
> Which they that know the rest, know more than I.

Until he was thirty, Herbert, though a devoted scholar and man of principle, lived happily enough among the 'flies of estates and sunshine'. His brother, Lord Herbert of Cherbury, a scholarly and upright man too, though something of an unbeliever, stayed all his life in this proud world. George Herbert, being sickly, was always closer to the reality of death. Like Donne, he warned mortality not to boast of its pride, as in his 'Dialogue-Anthem of the Christian and Death', but he saw death's proximity grimly enough.

> Death, thou wast once an uncouth hideous thing,
> Nothing but bones,
> The sad effect of sadder groans:
> Thy mouth was open, but thou couldst not sing.

Most readers are likely to find the last line of this stanza more convincing than the balm which follows, when Herbert reflects on Christ's sacrifice of his own life to save mankind from death.

> But since our Saviour's death did put some blood
> Into thy face;
> Thou art grown fair and full of grace,
> Much in request, much sought for, as a good.

> For we do now behold thee gay and glad,
> As at doomsday;
> When souls shall wear their new array,
> And all thy bones with beauty shall be clad.

> Therefore we can go die as sleep, and trust
> Half that we have
> Unto an honest faithful grave;
> Making our pillows either down, or dust.

It is Herbert's directness, amidst all his ingenious structuring, which speaks clearly to us today. We congratulate ourselves that we write wholly in the vernacular and not in some special poetic diction. But Herbert shames us by showing how to be blazingly direct while never threadbare or trivial. This directness extends to his handling of grammar, especially his way with verbs. He strikes in the space between one word and the next. The following is the complete text of his poem 'Praise I'.

> To write a verse or two, is all the praise,
> That I can raise:
> Mend my estate in any ways,
> Thou shalt have more.

> I go to Church, help me to wings, and I
> Will thither fly;
> Or, if I mount unto the sky,
> I will do more.

> Man is all weakness; there is no such thing
> As Prince or King:
> His arm is short; yet with a sling
> He may do more.

8

An herb distilled, and drunk, may dwell next door,
On the same floor,
To a brave soul: Exalt the poor,
They can do more.

O raise me then! Poor bees that work all day,
Sting my delay,
Who have work, as well as they,
And much, much more.

'Sting' is such a verb. There is no word in this poem of more than two syllables, yet the metaphysical pressure is high. Whether praise is our proper work as Christians Herbert does not debate. But even if it were not, his poem presses hard on that inborn impulse to make more of this life we have been given so mysteriously. 'Divine discontent' may be a hard concept to believe in today, but it suggests the ambiguous exchange between Hamlet and Rosencrantz and Guildenstern, especially Hamlet's speech, 'what a piece of work is a man ...' Is Hamlet satirizing Renaissance confidence or is he annotating it? By the same token, doesn't Herbert's poem take wing on its own ambiguity? The perfect God wants us to praise him, because that is proper work for the divine spirit in us. Language entices us and we want it to show us the heavens.

I doubt that there is a poem of Herbert's which is not both a pleasure and a surprise to read. For all his moral precision, he is beautifully various. As he faces the church year his gaze takes in the whole horizon of life. Coming to God and God's ordinances is not for Herbert some sort of 'Carthage must be destroyed' challenge imposed on the business of the day. He never forgets his role as intercessor.

Throw away thy rod,
Throw away thy wrath:
O my God,
Take the gentle path.

Stravinsky said that we should praise God with a little talent if we have any. In return he will give us his music and his stained glass and many other delights, which it would be the grossest Manicheism not to delight in.

But when thou dost anneal in glass thy story,
Making thy life to shine within

9

The holy Preacher's; then the light and glory
More reveren'd grows, and more doth win:
Which else show wat'rish, bleak and thin.

Doctrine and life, colours and light, in one
When they combine and mingle, bring
A strong regard and awe: but speech alone
Doth vanish like a flaring thing,
And in the ear, not conscience ring.

('The Windows')

And this is why speech has to be made into poetry, where it can begin to do its proper work in the same way that music and stained glass do theirs.

A reader of this study will observe that my introduction stresses different aspects of Herbert's genius from those set out by T. S. Eliot. But I disagree with nothing which Eliot propounds. Herbert, as presented by Eliot in 1962, was about to come into his kingdom. It was high time: he is one of the very greatest poets in the language. Following T. S. Eliot's argument is to be fired by a passion to read Herbert's poems immediately, or to read them all over again. He is a magician, and there is always a shortage of magic in our lives. Herbert puts it beautifully in one of his smallest and most winning poems, 'The Quiddity'.

My God, a verse is not a crown,
No point of honour, or gay suit,
No hawk, or banquet, or renown,
Nor a good sword, nor yet a lute.

It cannot vault, or dance, or play;
It never was in *France* or *Spain*;
Nor can it entertain the day
With a great stable or demesne.

It is not office, art, or news,
Not the Exchange, or busy Hall;
But it is that which while I use
I am with thee, and *Most take all*.

George Herbert

T. S. Eliot

1

Life and Background

The family background of a man of genius is always of interest. It may show evidence of powers which blaze forth in one member, or it may show no promise of superiority of any kind. Or it may, like that of George Herbert, show distinction of a very different order. There is a further reason for knowing something of the ancestry of George Herbert: it is of interest to us because it was important to him.

The family of Herbert was, and still is, notable among the British aristocracy. I say British rather than English, because one branch of the family, that to which the poet belonged, had established itself in Wales and had intermarried with Welsh landed families. The Herberts lay claim to being of Norman-French origin, and to having been land-holders since the Norman conquest. At the time of the Wars of the Roses the Herberts of Wales had supported the Yorkist cause; but after the battle of Bosworth they transferred their allegiance to the new monarch, the Lancastrian Henry Tudor, himself a Welshman on his father's side, who ascended the throne as Henry VII. Under the new dynasty the Herberts continued to flourish. Henry VII was determined to exert in Wales the same authority that he enjoyed in England – a control to which the local chieftains of Wales were not accustomed. Among those Welshmen of position and authority who supported and advanced King Henry's law and order in Wales was Sir Richard Herbert of Montgomery Castle. Montgomery lies in North Wales; in the South another Herbert was (and is) Earl of Pembroke; and still another branch of the family is represented by the Earl of Carnarvon.

George Herbert's ancestors and kinsmen were active both in the service of the King and in local affairs. Their rank was among the highest. Several of the family were distinguished for their courage, their prowess in war and duel and their astounding feats of arms. An exceptional race, but giving no indication of literary tastes and ability before the time of George Herbert and his brother Edward. That two poets, brothers, should appear in a family so conspicuous for warlike deeds, administrative gifts and attendance at court, can only be accounted for by the fact that their mother, the wife of Sir Richard Herbert of Montgomery, was a woman of literary tastes and of strong character and of exceptional gifts of mind as well as beauty and charm. She was Magdalen, daughter and heiress of Sir Richard Newport, a wealthy landowner in Shropshire.

George Herbert was born in 1593. Three years later his father died, leaving the mother with ten children, seven boys and three girls. Edward was the eldest son; the younger sons would have, of course, to make their own way in life – presumably, as other Herberts had done, in the wars or in some public service – but Lady Herbert's standards were high and she was determined to give them all a good education. The eldest, Edward, the other poet of the family and the heir to the estates, was thirteen and already an undergraduate at Oxford when his father died. At fifteen Edward was married off to an heiress (a Herbert of another branch) but continued at Oxford, where his mother moved her family to be near him and to supervise his education. There she had friends, and even held a kind of salon, among the more brilliant of the learned dons.

It is worth while to say something of Edward Herbert, the eldest brother, not merely to mention his poetry but to point the striking contrast between the two gifted brothers. Edward was ambitious to live abroad, to enjoy court life in foreign capitals and to engage in rather dilettante diplomacy; and to this end he learned French, Italian and Spanish. He seems to have been a man of great physical strength, and was noted for his address at sports and success in love-making: in short, he was a man of abounding vitality. He was later raised to the peerage as Lord Herbert of Cherbury, by which name he is known as author of at least two very fine poems familiar to readers of anthologies. He was not only a poet, but something of a philosopher, and entertained distinctly heretical views in religious matters. On the other hand, John Donne spoke well of him, and Ben Jonson was a friend and correspondent. For he enjoyed the society of men of letters, among whom he moved as an equal as well as among the courtiers of Europe and among ladies and gentlemen of fashion. In Edward the characteristic traits of the Herberts and some of the particular traits of Magdalen Herbert, his mother, appear to have been combined. In George, of frailer constitution and contemplative mind, we seem to find more of Magdalen; yet he was as proudly conscious of being a Herbert as any other Herbert, and at one period had the family inclination to life in the world of public affairs.

By far the most important for our study of George Herbert, of the men of letters and the scholars who delighted in the company of Magdalen Herbert, was John Donne. He was enough older in years to have the admiration of the younger man and to influence him: he was enough beneath Lady Herbert in rank to be almost a protégé. The friendship between Donne and Lady Herbert is commemorated in one of Donne's best known and most loved poems, 'The Autumnal', in which is found the couplet which every lover of Donne's poetry knows by heart:

> No Spring, nor Summer Beauty hath such grace
> As I have seen in one autumnal face.

To the influence of Donne's poetry upon that of Herbert we shall return presently. Meanwhile it is in place to provide a brief survey of Herbert's life and a sketch of his character.

At the age of twelve George Herbert was sent to Westminster School, where he became proficient in the usual disciplines of Latin and Greek, and gained also – what is equally important for mention here – an advanced practice in music: not only in the choral singing for which that famous school was well known because of its association with the services in Westminster Abbey, but also with a difficult instrument – the lute. If we remember Herbert's knowledge of music, and his skill at the instrument, we appreciate all the better his mastery of lyric verse. From Westminster he went on to Trinity College, Cambridge, being one of the three boys of Westminster School who were given scholarships to that College at that time.

At Westminster School Herbert had an exemplary record. The relation of the school to the Abbey had also familiarized him with the church offices, in which the boys took part. (Their close attention to the sermon was ensured by the requirement that they should afterwards compose a summary of it in Latin.) At the university

Herbert was equally forward; sober and staid in his conduct and diligent in his studies, he was given particular attention by the Master. It was said of him, however, that he was careful to be well, even expensively dressed; and that his attitude towards his fellow undergraduates of lower social position was distant, if not supercilious. Even Isaac Walton (his most nearly contemporary biographer), who tends to emphasize Herbert's saintliness, admits that Herbert, at this stage of his life, was very much aware of the consideration which he thought due to his exalted birth.

At the age of twenty-three Herbert was made a Fellow of his own college of Trinity. He began by instructing the younger undergraduates in Greek grammar; later he taught rhetoric and the rules of oratory. His health was never good; and the climate of Cambridge was somewhat harsh for a young man of frail constitution. His income as Fellow and Tutor was eked out by a small allowance from his brother Edward (the head of the family) and occasionally by gifts from his step-father. For his mother had, in middle age, married again, and was now the wife of Sir John Danvers. But Herbert's poor health meant doctors' bills and occasional absences from Cambridge; as a learned scholar of an active and curious mind he needed constantly to purchase books, and books were expensive, especially those which had to be imported from the continent. He therefore sought to improve his finances, and at the same time attain a position of considerable dignity, by obtaining appointment as Public Orator to the University.

Herbert had not yet formed the design of passing his life as a country parson. Indeed, the post of Public Orator was one which would bring him into the great world and even into contact with the court of James I. He achieved his aim; and during his tenure of this office acquired an extensive acquaintance, which his family connections and his own wide sympathies helped to enlarge. He greatly admired Sir Francis Bacon, a man of a type of mind very different from his own; another elder friend with whom he was on affectionate terms was the saintly Bishop Lancelot Andrewes. Nor did a wide divergence of religious attitude and belief diminish the warm regard between him and his elder brother Edward.

A Fellow of a College was expected to take holy orders in the Church of England within seven years of his appointment, or resign his Fellowship. Herbert was, like his mother, a practising and devout Anglican, but at this time his ambition looked toward the world of Court and Government. His violent attack, in the form of a Latin thesis, upon the Puritan position in the person of one of its most outrageous zealots, Andrew Melville, was his only sortie into religious controversy; though undoubtedly wholly sincere, Herbert probably aimed at winning the approval of King James. He would certainly have liked public office, but had neither the wiles of ingratiation, nor the means or the wish to buy his way in. His next step was to become a Member of Parliament for Montgomery – an election which came to him almost as a matter of course as a member of the Herbert family. But this period of his life was not marked by success; two great noblemen of whose patronage he felt assured died, and the death of King James himself, in the following year, seems to have left him with little hope of a Secretaryship of State.

It was necessary to review this much of Herbert's early life to make the point that Herbert, though from childhood a pious member of the Anglican Church, and a vigorous opponent of the Puritans and Calvinists, felt no strong vocation to the priesthood until his thirty-first year. There were at least four persons in his life who may, by precept or example, have influenced him to this decision. His mother, to whom he was devotedly attached, was, we know, a woman not only of strong character, but of great piety. Two friends much older than himself have already been mentioned: Dr John Donne and Bishop Andrewes. And finally, there was his dear friend Nicholas Ferrar of Little Gidding, an exemplar of High Churchmanship, whose domestic life approached that of a religious community. To Ferrar it was that he consigned, upon his death, the manuscript collection of verse upon which his fame is founded, the collection *The Temple* which we should not know had Ferrar not chosen to publish it; this he did in the same year in which Herbert died.[1]

Herbert's mother died in 1626. George Herbert was for a time a guest in the house of his step-father's elder brother, Lord Danvers, and in 1629, having already taken holy orders, he married Jane Danvers, the daughter of a cousin of Lord Danvers. It was a happy marriage. Six years after Herbert's death, his widow married Sir Robert Cook. In her widowhood, Isaac Walton says:

> She continued mourning, till time and conversation had so moderated her sorrows, that she became the happy wife of Sir Robert Cook of Highnam in the County of Gloucester, Knight. And though he put a

high value on the excellent accomplishments of her mind and body; and was so like Mr Herbert, as not to govern like a Master, but as an affectionate Husband; yet she would even to him take occasion to mention the name of Mr George Herbert, and say that name must live in her memory, till she put off mortality.

George Herbert died of consumption at the age of forty. For the last years of his life he had been Rector of the parish of Bemerton in Wiltshire. That he was an exemplary parish priest, strict in his own observances and a loving and generous shepherd of his flock, there is ample testimony, And we should bear in mind that, at the time when Herbert lived, it was most unusual that a man of George Herbert's social position should take orders and be content to devote himself to the spiritual and material needs of a small parish of humble folk in a rural village. From Walton's *Life* I must quote one anecdote:

In another walk to *Salisbury*, he saw a poor man, with a poorer horse, that was fall'n under his Load; they were both in distress, and needed present help; which Mr *Herbert* perceiving, put off his Canonical Coat, and help'd the poor man to unload, and after, to lead his horse: The poor man blest him for it: and he blest the poor man; and was so like the *good Samaritan* that he gave him money to refresh both himself and his horse: and told him, *That if he lov'd himself, he should be merciful to his Beast.* Thus he left the poor man, and at his coming to his musical friends at *Salisbury*, they began to wonder that Mr *George Herbert* which us'd to be so trim and clean, came into the company so soyl'd and discompos'd; but he told them the occasion: And when one of the company told him, *He had disparag'd himself by so dirty an employment;* his answer was, *That the thought of what he had done, would prove Musick to him at Midnight; and that the omission of it would have upbraided and made discord in his Conscience, whensoever he should pass by that place; for, if I be bound to pray for all that be in distress, I am sure that I am bound so far as it is in my power to practise what I pray for. And though I do not wish for the like occasion every day, let me tell you, I would not willingly pass one day of my life without comforting a sad soul, or shewing mercy; and I praise God for this occasion:* And now let's tune our instruments.

In this context is worth mention a prose treatise of Herbert's entitled *A Priest to the Temple, Or, The Country Parson His Character etc.* In this treatise he sets forth the duties and responsibilities of the country parson to God, to his flock, and to himself; and from what we know of Herbert we can be sure that he practised, and always strove to practise, what he here prescribes to other priests.

The story of the poor man and his horse is all the more touching when we read that the Parson's apparel should be

> plaine, but reverend, and clean, without spots, or dust, or smell; the purity of his mind breaking out, and dilating it selfe even to his body, cloaths, and habitation.

We are told elsewhere in the same treatise that a priest who serves as domestic chaplain to some great person is not to be

> over-submissive, and base, but to keep up with the Lord and Lady of the house, and to preserve a boldness with them and all, even so farre as reproofe to their very face, when occasion calls, but seasonably and discreetly.

The pride of birth natural to Herbert is transformed into the dignity of the Servant of God. The parson, he continues, should be a man of wide reading: Herbert mentions the Church Fathers and the Scholastics, and tells us that the parson should be attentive to later writers also. The parson must give careful attention to his sermon, taking due account of the needs and capacities of his parishioners, and keeping their attention by persuading them that his sermon is addressed to this particular congregation and to one and all of them. And he should, especially when visiting the sick, or otherwise afflicted, persuade them to particular confession, 'labouring to make them understand the great good use of this antient and pious ordinance'.

We are not to presume, however, that George Herbert was naturally of a meek and mild disposition. He was, on the contrary somewhat haughty; proud of his descent and social position; and, like others of his family, of a quick temper. In his poems we can find ample evidence of his spiritual struggles, of self-examination and self-criticism, and of the cost at which he acquired godliness.

> I struck the board, and cry'd, No more.
> I will abroad.
> What? shall I ever sigh and pine?
> My lines and life are free; free as the rode,
> Loose as the winde, as large as store.
> Shall I be still in suit?
> Have I no harvest but a thorn
> To let me bloud, and not restore
> What I have lost with cordiall fruit?
> Sure there was wine

Before my sighs did drie it: there was corn
　　Before my tears did drown it.
　　Is the yeare onely lost to me?
　　　　Have I no bayes to crown it?
No flowers, no garlands gay? all blasted?
　　　　All wasted?
Not so, my heart: but there is fruit
　　　　And thou hast hands.
Recover all thy sigh-blown age
On double pleasures: leave thy cold dispute
Of what is fit and not. Forsake thy cage,
　　　　Thy rope of sands,
Which pettie thoughts have made, and made to thee
　　Good cable, to enforce and draw,
　　　　And be thy law,
　　While thou didst wink and wouldst not see.
　　　　Away; take heed;
　　　　I will abroad.
Call in thy deaths head there: tie up thy fears.
　　　　He that forbears
　　　　To suit and serve his need
　　　　Deserves his load.
But as I rav'd and grew more fierce and wilde
　　　　At every word,
Me thoughts I heard one calling, *Child!*
　　And I reply'd, *My Lord.*

('The Collar')

To think of Herbert as the poet of a placid and comfortable easy piety is to misunderstand utterly the man and his poems. Yet such was the impression of Herbert and of the Church of England given by the critic who wrote the introduction to the World's Classics edition of Herbert's poems in 1907. For this writer, the Church of England, in Herbert's day as well as in his own, is typified by a peaceful country churchyard in the late afternoon:

Here, as the cattle wind homeward in the evening light, the benign, white-haired parson stands at his gate to greet the cowherd, and the village chimes call the labourers to evensong. For these contented spirits, happily removed from the stress and din of contending creeds and clashing dogmas, the message of the gospel tells of divine approval for work well done ... And among these typical spirits, beacons of a quiet hope, no figure stands out more brightly or more memorably than that of George Herbert.

This rustic scene belongs to the world of Tennyson and Dickens; but no more to the world of George Herbert than to our world today. It is well that the latest World's Classics edition (the text based on that established by F. E. Hutchinson) has a new introduction by the learned and sensitive critic, Miss Helen Gardner. The earlier introduction gave a false picture both of Herbert and his poetry, and of the Church itself in an age of bitter religious conflict and passionate theology: it is worth quoting in order to point out how false a picture this is.

2

The Temple

The poems on which George Herbert's reputation is based are those constituting the collection called *The Temple*. About *The Temple* there are two points to be made. The first is that we cannot date the poems exactly. Some of them may be the product of careful re-writing. We cannot take them as being necessarily in chronological order: they have another order, that in which Herbert wished them to be read. *The Temple* is, in fact, a structure, and one which may have been worked over and elaborated, perhaps at intervals of time, before it reached its final form. We cannot judge Herbert, or savour fully his genius and his art, by any selection to be found in an anthology; we must study *The Temple* as a whole.

To understand Shakespeare we must acquaint ourselves with all of his plays; to understand Herbert we must acquaint ourselves with all of *The Temple*. Herbert is, of course, a much slighter poet than Shakespeare; nevertheless he may justly be called a major poet. Yet even in anthologies he has for the most part been underrated. In Sir Arthur Quiller-Couch's *Oxford Book of English Verse*, which was for many years unchallenged in its representative character, George Herbert was allotted five pages – the same number as Bishop King and much less than Robert Herrick, the latter of whom, most critics of today would agree, is a poet of very much slighter gifts. For poetic range Herbert was commonly considered more limited than Donne; and for intensity he was compared unfavourably with Crashaw. This is the view even of Professor Grierson, to whom we are greatly indebted for his championship of Donne and of those poets whose names are associated with that of Donne.

And here we must exercise caution in our interpretation of the phrase 'the school of Donne'. The present writer once contemplated writing a book under that title; and lately the title has been used by a distinguished younger critic [A. Alvarez] for a study covering the same ground. The phrase is legitimate and useful to designate that generation of men younger than Donne whose work is obviously influenced by him, but we must not take it as implying that those poets who experienced his influence were for that reason lesser poets. (Professor Grierson, indeed, seems to consider Andrew Marvell the greatest, greater even than Donne.) That Herbert learned directly from Donne is self-evident. But to think of 'the school of Donne', otherwise 'the metaphysical poets', as Donne's inferiors, or to try to range them on a scale of greatness, would be to lose our way. What is important is to apprehend the particular virtue, the unique flavour of each one. Comparing them with any other group of poets at any other period, we observe the characteristics which they share: when we compare them with each other, their differences emerge clearly.

Let us compare a poem by Donne with a poem by Herbert; and as Herbert's poetry deals always with religious matter, we shall compare two religious sonnets. First, Donne:

Batter my heart, three person'd God; for, you
As yet but knocke, breathe, shine, and seeke to mend;
That I may rise, and stand, o'erthrow mee,'and bend
Your force, to breake, blowe, burn and make me new.
I, like an usurpt towne, to'another due,
Labour to 'admit you, but Oh, to no end,
Reason your viceroy in mee, mee shall defend,
But is captiv'd, and proves weake or untrue.
Yet dearely'I love you,'and would be loved faine,
But am betroth'd unto your enemie:
Divorce mee,'untie, or break that knot againe;
Take mee to you, imprison mee, for I
Except you'enthrall mee, never shall be free,
Nor ever chast, except you ravish mee.

And here is George Herbert:

PRAYER (I)
Prayer the Churches banquet, Angels age,
Gods breath in man returning to his birth,
The soul in paraphrase, heart in pilgrimage,
The Christian plummet sounding heav'n and earth;
Engine against th' Almightie, sinners towre,

23

Reversed thunder, Christ-side-piercing spear,
The six-daies world transposing in an houre,
A kinde of tune, which all things heare and fear;
Softnesse, and peace, and joy, and love, and blisse,
Exalted Manna, gladnesse of the best,
Heaven in ordinarie, man well drest,
The milkie way, the bird of Paradise,
Church-bels beyond the starres heard, the souls bloud,
The land of spices; something understood.

The difference that I wish to emphasize is not that between the violence of Donne and the gentle imagery of Herbert, but rather a difference between the dominance of sensibility over intellect. Both men were highly intellectual, both men had very keen sensibility: but in Donne thought seems in control of feeling, and in Herbert feeling seems in control of thought. Both men were learned, both men were accustomed to preaching – but not to the same type of congregation. In Donne's religious verse, as in his sermons, there is much more of the *orator*: whereas Herbert, for all that he had been successful as Public Orator of Cambridge University, has a much more intimate tone of speech. We do not know what Herbert's sermons were like; but we can conjecture that in addressing his little congregation of rustics, all of whom he knew personally, and many of whom must have received both spiritual and material comfort from him and from his wife, he adopted a more homely style. Donne was accustomed to addressing large congregations (one is tempted to call them 'audiences') out of doors at Paul's Cross, Herbert only the local congregation of a village church.

The difference which I have in mind is indicated even by the last two lines of each sonnet. Donne's

> ... for I
> Except you'enthrall mee, never shall be free,
> Nor ever chast, except you ravish mee

is, in the best sense, *wit*. Herbert's

> Church-bels beyond the starres heard, the souls bloud,
> The land of spices, something understood

is the kind of poetry which, like

> magic casements, opening on the foam
> Of perilous seas, in faery lands forlorn

24

may be called *magical*.

Of all the poets who may be said to belong to 'the school of Donne', Herbert is the only one whose whole source of inspiration was his religious faith. Most of the poetry upon which rests the reputation of Donne is love poetry, and his religious verse is of a later period in his life; his reputation, and his influence upon other poets would have been as great had he written no religious poetry at all. Richard Crashaw, who had himself frequented the community of Nicholas Ferrar at Little Gidding before his conversion to the Church of Rome, might still have been a notable poet had he written no religious verse – even though his devotional poems are his finest. Herbert, before becoming Rector of Bemerton, had never been a recluse: he had, in his short life, wide acquaintance in the great world, and he enjoyed a happy marriage. Yet it was only in the Faith, in hunger and thirst after godliness, in his self-questioning and his religious meditation, that he was inspired as a poet. If there is another example since his time of a poetic genius so dedicated to God, it is that of Gerard Hopkins. We are certainly justified in presuming that no other subject matter than that to which he confined himself could have elicited great poetry from George Herbert. Whether we regard this as a limitation, or as the sign of solitary greatness, of a unique contribution to English poetry, will depend upon our sensibility to the themes of which he writes.

It would, however, be a gross error to assume that Herbert's poems are of value only for Christians – or, still more narrowly, only for members of his own church. For the practising Christian, it is true, they may be aids to devotion. When I claim a place for Herbert among those poets whose work every lover of English poetry should read and every student of English poetry should study, irrespective of religious belief or unbelief, I am not thinking primarily of the exquisite craftmanship, the extraordinary metrical virtuosity, or the verbal felicities, but of the *content* of the poems which make up *The Temple*. These poems form a record of spiritual struggle which should touch the feeling, and enlarge the understanding of those readers also who hold no religious belief and find themselves unmoved by religious emotion. Professor L. C. Knights, in an essay on George Herbert in his *Explorations*, both expresses this doubt on the part of the non-Christian and dispels it:

Even Dr Hutchinson, whose superbly edited and annotated edition of the Complete Works is not likely to be superseded ... remarks that 'if to-day there is a less general sympathy with Herbert's religion, the beauty and sincerity of its expression are appreciated by those who do not share it'. True, but there is much more than the 'expression' that we appreciate, as I shall try to show. Herbert's poetry is an integral part of the great English tradition.

Whether the religious poems of Donne show greater profundity of thought, and great intensity of passion, is a question which every reader will answer according to his own feelings. My point here is that *The Temple* is not to be regarded simply as a collection of poems, but (as I have said) as a record of the spiritual struggles of a man of intellectual power and emotional intensity who gave much toil to perfecting his verses. As such, it should be a document of interest to all those who are curious to understand their fellow men; and as such, I regard it as a more important document than all of Donne's *religious* poems taken together.

On the other hand, I find Herbert to be closer in spirit to Donne than is any other of 'the school of Donne'. As the personal bond, through Lady Herbert, was much closer, this seems only natural. Other powerful literary influences formed the manner of Crashaw, the Roman Catholic convert: the Italian poet Marino and the Spanish poet Gongora, and, we are told,[2] the Jesuit poets who wrote in Latin. Vaughan and Traherne were poets of mystical experience: each appears to have experienced early in life some mystical illumination which inspires his poetry. And the other important poet of the 'metaphysical' school, Andrew Marvell, is a master of secular and religious poetry equally. In my attempt to indicate the affinity of Herbert to Donne, and also the difference between them, I have spoken earlier of a 'balance' between the intellect and the sensibility. But equally well (for one has recourse to diverse and even mutually contradictory metaphors and images to express the inexpressible) we can speak of a 'fusion' of intellect and sensibility in different proportions. In the work of a later generation of 'metaphysicals' – notably Cleveland, Benlowes and Cowley – we encounter a kind of emotional drought, and a verbal ingenuity which, having no great depth of feeling to work upon, tends towards corruption of language, and merits the censure which Samuel Johnson applies indiscriminately to all the 'school of Donne'.

To return to the import of *The Temple* for all perceptive readers whether they share Herbert's faith or no, Professor Knights quotes with approval Dr Hutchinson's description of the poems as

> colloquies of the soul with God or self-communings which seek to bring order into that complex personality of his which he analyses so unsparingly,

but goes on to make a qualification which seems to me very important. Dr Hutchinson believes that Herbert's principal temptation was *ambition*. We need not deny that Herbert had been, like many other men, ambitious; we know that he had a hot temper; we know that he liked fine clothes and fine company, and would have been pleased by preferment at Court. But beside the struggle to abandon thought of the attractions offered to worldly ambition, Professor Knights finds 'a dejection of spirit that tended to make him regard his own life, the life he was actually leading, as worthless and unprofitable'. Mr Knights attributes the cause partly to ill-health, but still more to a *more ingrained distrust*. It was perhaps distrust of himself, or fear of testing his powers among more confident men, that drove him to the shelter of an obscure parsonage. He had, Mr Knights suggests, to rid himself of the torturing sense of frustration and impotence and accept the validity of his own experience. If this is so, Herbert's weakness became the source of his greatest power, for the result was *The Temple*.

I have called upon Mr Knights's testimony in evidence that Herbert is not a poet whose work is significant only for Christian readers; that *The Temple* is not to be taken as simply a devotional handbook of meditation for the faithful, but as the personal record of a man very conscious of weakness and failure, a man of intellect and sensibility who hungered and thirsted after righteousness. And that by its *content*, as well as because of its technical accomplishment, it is a work of importance for every lover of poetry. This is not, however, to suggest that it is unprofitable for us to study the text for closer understanding, to acquaint ourselves with the liturgy of the Church, with the traditional imagery of the Church, and identify the Biblical allusions. One long poem which has been subjected to close examination is 'The Sacrifice'. There are sixty-three stanzas of three lines each, sixty-one of which have the refrain 'Was ever grief like mine?' I mention this poem, which is a very fine one, and not so familiar as are some of the shorter and more lyrical pieces, because it has been carefully studied by Professor William Empson in his *Seven*

Types of Ambiguity, and by Miss Rosamund Tuve in her *A Reading of George Herbert.* The lines are to be taken as spoken by Christ upon the Cross. We need, of course, enough acquaintance with the New Testament to recognize references to the Passion. But we are also better prepared if we recognize the Lamentations of Jeremiah, and the Reproaches in the Mass of the Presanctified which is celebrated on Good Friday.

> *Celebrant:* I led thee forth out of Egypt, drowning Pharaoh in the Red Sea: and thou hast delivered me up unto the chief priests.
> *Deacon & Subdeacon:* O my people, what have I done unto thee, or wherein have I wearied thee? Testify against me.

It is interesting to note that Mr Empson and Miss Tuve differ in their interpretation of the following stanza:

> O all ye who passe by, behold and see;
> Man stole the fruit, but I must climbe the tree;
> The tree of life to all, but onely me:
> > Was ever grief like mine?

Mr Empson comments: 'He climbs the tree to repay what was stolen, as if he were putting the apple back': and develops this explanation at some length. Upon this interpretation Miss Tuve observes rather tartly: 'All (Mr Empson's) rabbits roll out of one small hat – the fact that Herbert uses the time-honoured "climb" for the ascent of the Cross, and uses the world "must", to indicate a far deeper necessity than that which faces a small boy under a big tree'. Certainly, the image of *replacing* the apple which has been plucked is too ludicrous to be entertained for a moment. It is obvious that Christ 'climbs' or is 'lifted' up on the Cross in atonement for the sin of Adam and Eve; the verb 'climb' being used traditionally to indicate the *voluntary* nature of the sacrifice for the sins of the world. Herbert was, assuredly, familiar with the imagery used by the pre-Reformation Church. It is likely also that Donne, learned in the works of the scholastics, and also in the writings of such Roman theologians contemporary with himself as Cardinal Bellarmine, set a standard of scholarship which Herbert followed.

To cite such an instance as this, however, is not to suggest that the lover of poetry needs to prepare himself with theological and liturgical knowledge *before* approaching Herbert's poetry. That would be to put the cart before the horse. With the appreciation of

Herbert's poems, as with all poetry, enjoyment is the beginning as well as the end. We must enjoy the poetry before we attempt to penetrate the poet's mind; we must enjoy it before we understand it, if the attempt to understand it is to be worth the trouble. We begin by enjoying poems, and lines in poems, which make an immediate impression; only gradually, as we familiarize ourselves with the whole work, do we appreciate *The Temple* as a coherent sequence of poems setting down the fluctuations of emotion between despair and bliss, between agitation and serenity, and the discipline of suffering which leads to peace of spirit.

The relation of enjoyment to belief – the question whether a poem has more to give us if we share the beliefs of its author, is one which has never been answered satisfactorily: the present writer has made some attempt to contribute to the solution of the problem, and remains dissatisfied with his attempts. But one thing is certain: that even if the reader enjoys a poem more fully when he shares the beliefs of the author, he will miss a great deal of possible enjoyment and of valuable experience if he does not seek the fullest understanding possible of poetry in reading which he must 'suspend his disbelief'. (The present writer is very thankful for having had the opportunity to study the *Bhagavad Gītā* and the religious and philosophical beliefs, so different from his own, with which the *Bhagavad Gītā* is informed.)

Some of the poems in *The Temple* express moods of anguish and sense of defeat or failure:

> At first thou gav'st me milk and sweetnesses;
>   I had my wish and way:
> My dayes were straw'd with flow'rs and happinesse;
>   There was no moneth but May.
> But with my yeares sorrow did twist and grow,
> And made a partie unawares for wo. . . .
>
> Yet though thou troublest me, I must be meek;
>   In weaknesse must be stout.
> Well, I will change the service, and go seek
>   Some other master out.
> Ah my deare God! though I am clean forgot,
> Let me not love thee, if I love thee not.

The foregoing lines are from the first of five poems all of which bear the title 'Affliction'. In the first of two poems both of which are entitled 'The Temper', he speaks of his fluctuations of faith and feeling:

> How should I praise thee, Lord! how should my rymes
> Gladly engrave my love in steel,
> If what my soul doth feel sometimes,
> My soul might ever feel!

The great danger, for the poet who would write religious verse, is that of setting down what he would like to feel rather than being faithful to the expression of what he really feels. Of such pious insincerity Herbert is never guilty. We need not look too narrowly for a steady progress in Herbert's religious life, in an attempt to discover a chronological order. He falls, and rises again. Also, he was accustomed to working over his poems; they may have circulated in manuscript among his intimates during his lifetime. What we can confidently believe is that every poem in the book is true to the poet's experience. In some poems there is a more joyous note, as in 'Whitsunday':

> Listen sweet Dove unto my song,
> And spread thy golden wings in me;
> Hatching my tender heart so long,
> Till it get wing, and flie away with thee....
>
> Lord, though we change, thou art the same;
> The same sweet God of love and light:
> Restore this day, for thy great name,
> Unto his ancient and miraculous right.

In 'The Flower' we hear the note of serenity, almost of beatitude, and of thankfulness for God's blessings:

> How fresh, O Lord, how sweet and clean
> Are thy returns! ev'n as the flowers in spring;
> To which, besides their own demean,
> The late-past frosts tributes of pleasure bring.
> Grief melts away
> Like snow in May,
> As if there were no such cold thing.
>
> · · · · · ·
>
> And now in age I bud again,
> After so many deaths I live and write;
> I once more smell the dew and rain,
> And relish versing: O my onely light,
> It cannot be

That I am he
On whom thy tempests fell all night.[3]

I cannot resist the thought that in this last stanza – itself a miracle of phrasing – the imagery, so apposite to express the achievement of faith which it records, is taken from the experience of the man of delicate physical health who had known much illness. It is on this note of joy in convalescence of the spirit in surrender to God, that the life of discipline of this haughty and irascible Herbert finds conclusion: *In His will is our peace.*

3

Herbert and Donne

Of all the 'school of Donne' Herbert is the closest to the old Master. Two other fine poets of the group might just as well be said to belong to the 'school of Herbert'. The debt of Vaughan to Herbert can be shown by quotation; Herbert's most recent and authoritative editor, Dr F. E. Hutchinson, says: 'There is no example in English literature of one poet adopting another poet's work so extensively.' As for Crashaw, he undoubtedly admired Herbert. Nevertheless, in spite of a continuity of influence and inspiration, we must remember that these four poets, who form a constellation of religious genius unparalleled in English poetry, are all highly individual, and very different from each other.

The resemblances and differences between Donne and Herbert are peculiarly fascinating. I have suggested earlier that the difference between the poetry of Donne and Herbert shows some parallel to the difference between their careers in the Church. Donne the Dean of St Paul's, whose sermons drew crowds in the City of London; Herbert the shepherd of a little flock of rustics, to whom he laboured to explain the meaning of the rites of the Church, the significance of Holy Days, in language that they could understand. There are, however, lines which might have come from either, where we seem to hear the same voice – Herbert echoing the idiom or reflecting the imagery of Donne. There is at least one poem of Herbert's in which he plays with extended metaphor in the manner of Donne. It is 'Obedience' where he uses legal terms almost throughout:

> My God, if writings may
> Convey a Lordship any way
> Whither the buyer and the seller please;
> Let it not thee displease,
> If this poore paper do as much as they.

32

. . . . . .

He that will passe his land,
As I have mine, may set his hand
And heart unto this Deed, when he hath read;
And make the purchase spread
To both our goods, if he to it will stand.

Such elaboration is not typical of Herbert. But there is *wit* like that of Donne in 'The Quip'. One feels obliged to quote the whole poem:

The merrie world did on a day
With his train-bands and mates agree
To meet together, where I lay,
And all in sport to geere at me.

First, Beautie crept into a rose,
Which when I pluckt not, Sir, said she,
Tell me, I pray, Whose hands are those?
But thou shalt answer, Lord, for me.

Then Money came, and clinking still,
What tune is this, poore man? said he:
I heard in Musick you had skill.
But thou shalt answer, Lord, for me.

Then came brave Glorie puffing by
In silks that whistled, who but he?
He scarce allow'd me half an eie.
But thou shalt answer, Lord, for me.

Then came quick Wit and Conversation,
And he would needs a comfort be,
And, to be short, make an Oration.
But thou shalt answer, Lord, for me.

Yet when the houre of thy designe
To answer these fine things shall come;
Speak not at large; say, I am thine:
And then they have their answer home.

Professor Knights observes very shrewdly: 'the personifications here have nothing in common with Spenser's allegorical figures or with the capitalised abstractions of the eighteenth century: "brave Glorie puffing by in silks that whistled" might have come straight from *The Pilgrim's Progress*.' How audible are these silks 'that whistled'! 'Puffing' is equally apt: the same participle is used, to produce another but equally striking effect, elsewhere:

33

> Sometimes Death, puffing at the doore,
> Blows all the dust about the floore.
>
> ('The Church Floore')

Herbert is a master of the simple everyday word in the right place,
and charges it with concentrated meaning, as in 'Redemption', one
of the poems known to all readers of anthologies:

> Having been tenant long to a rich Lord,
> Not thriving, I resolved to be bold,
> And make a suit unto him, to afford
> A new small-rented lease, and cancell th'old.
> In heaven at his manour I him sought:
> They told me there, that he was lately gone
> About some land, which he had dearly bought
> Long since on earth, to take possession.
> I straight return'd, and knowing his great birth,
> Sought him accordingly in great resorts;
> In cities, theatres, gardens, parks, and courts:
> At length I heard a ragged noise and mirth
> Of theeves and murderers: there I him espied,
> Who straight, *Your suit is granted*, said, & died.

The phrase 'ragged noise and mirth' gives us, in four words, the
picture of the scene to which Herbert wishes to introduce us.
There are many lines which remind us of Donne:

> What though my bodie runne to dust?
> Faith cleaves unto it, counting ev'ry grain
> With an exact and most particular trust,
> Reserving all for flesh again.
>
> ('Faith')

> My God, what is a heart?
> Silver, or gold, or precious stone,
> Or starre, or rainbow, or a part
> Of all these things, or all of them in one?
>
> ('Mattens')

> ... learn here thy stemme
> And true descent; that when thou shalt grow fat,
>
> And wanton in thy cravings, thou mayst know,
> That flesh is but the glasse, which holds the dust
> That measures all our time; which also shall
> Be crumbled into dust ...
>
> ('Church-monuments')

34

Lord, how can man preach thy eternall word?
He is a brittle crazie glasse ...
('The Windows')

My bent thoughts, like a brittle bow,
Did flie asunder ...
('Deniall')

Herbert must have learned from Donne the cunning use of both
the learned and the common word, to give the sudden shock of
surprise and delight.

But man is close, reserv'd, and dark to thee:
When thou demandest but a heart,
He cavils instantly.
In his poor cabinet of bone
Sinnes have their box apart,
Defrauding thee, who gavest two for one.
('Ungratefulnesse')

The fleet Astronomer can bore,
And thred the sphere with his quick-piercing minde:
He views their stations, walks from doore to doore,
Surveys, as if he had design'd
To make a purchase there: he sees their dances,
And knoweth long before
Both their full-ey'd aspects, and secret glances.
('Vanitie')

My thoughts are all a case of knives ...
('Affliction IV')

The following lines are very reminiscent of Donne:

How soon doth man decay!
When clothes are taken from a chest of sweets
To swaddle infants, whose young breath
Scarce knows the way;
Those clouts are little winding sheets,
Which do consigne and send them unto death.
('Mortification')

Here and there one can believe that Herbert has unconsciously
used a word, or a rhyme of Donne, in a very different context from
that of the original, as perhaps in the first line of 'The Discharge':

Busie enquiring heart, what wouldst thou know?

Donne begins 'The Sunne Rising' with the line

> Busie old foole, unruly Sunne ...

If Herbert's line be an echo and not a mere coincidence – the reader must form his own opinion – it is all the more interesting because of the difference in subject matter between the two poems. If Herbert, in writing a poem of religious *mortification*, could echo a poem of Donne which is an *aubade* of the lover's complaint that day should come so soon, it suggests that the literary influence of the elder man upon the younger was profound indeed.

Herbert's metrical forms, however, are both original and varied. To have invented and perfected so many variations in the form of lyrical verse is evidence of native genius, hard work and a passion for perfection. Two of his poems are such as would be considered, if written by a poet today, merely elegant trifles: 'The Altar' and 'Easter Wings'. In each, there is a disposition of longer and shorter lines so printed that the poem has the shape, the one of an altar and the other of a pair of wings. Such a diversion, if employed frequently, would be tedious, distracting and trying to the eyesight and we must be glad that Herbert did not make further use of these devices; yet it is evidence of Herbert's care for workmanship, his restless exploration of variety, and of a kind of gaiety of spirit, a joy in composition which engages our delighted sympathy. The exquisite variations of form in the other poems of *The Temple* show a resourcefulness of invention which seems inexhaustible, and for which I know no parallel in English poetry. Here, we can only quote a stanza from each of a brief selection to suggest the astonishing variety:

> O my chief good,
> How shall I measure out thy bloud?
> How shall I count what thee befell,
> And each grief tell?
>
> ('Good Friday')

> O blessed bodie! Whither art thou thrown?
> No lodging for thee, but a cold hard stone?
> So many hearts on earth, and yet not one
> Receive thee?
>
> ('Sepulchre')

Poems in such measures as these, and more obviously 'The Sacrifice', which we have quoted earlier, seem to indicate an ear trained by the music of liturgy.

> Rise heart; thy Lord is risen. Sing his praise
> Without delayes,
> Who takes thee by the hand, that thou likewise
> With him mayst rise:
> That, as his death calcined thee to dust,
> His life may make thee gold, and much more, just.
>
> ('Easter')

The slow movement of the last line quoted above has something of the movement of the exquisite line which ends Donne's 'Nocturnall upon S. Lucies Day':

> Both the yeares, and the dayes deep midnight is.

Somewhat similar to the movement of 'Good Friday' (quoted above) is:

> Since, Lord, to thee
> A narrow way and little gate
> Is all the passage, on my infancie
> Thou didst lay hold, and antedate
> My faith in me.
>
> ('Holy Baptisme I')

Close enough to the form of 'Holy Baptisme' for its difference to be all the more striking is:

> Lord, I confesse my sinne is great;
> Great is my sinne. Oh! gently treat
> With thy quick flow'r, thy momentarie bloom;
> Whose life still pressing
> Is one undressing,
> A steadie aiming at a tombe.
>
> ('Repentance')

The next quotation has a solemn liturgical movement suited to the subject matter and the title:

> O Do not use me
> After my sinnes! look not on my desert,
> But on thy glorie! then thou wilt reform
> And not refuse me: for thou onely art
> The mightie God, but I a sillie worm;
> O do not bruise me!
>
> ('Sighs and Grones')

Herbert knows the effect of denying a rhyme where it is expected:

> When my devotions could not pierce
> Thy silent eares;
> Then was my heart broken, as was my verse:
> My breast was full of fears
> And disorder ...

('Deniall')

The roughness of the metre of the line

> Then was my heart broken, as was my verse

is exactly what is wanted to convey the meaning of the words. The following stanza has an apparent artlessness and conversational informality which only a great artist could achieve:

> Lord, let the Angels praise thy name.
> Man is a foolish thing, a foolish thing,
> Folly and Sinne play all his game.
> His house still burns, and yet he still doth sing,
> *Man is but grasse,*
> *He knows it, fill the glasse.*

('Miserie')

The next poem to be quoted is one of several poems of Herbert which, while being, like all the rest of his work, personal, have been set to music and sung as hymns:

> King of Glorie, King of Peace,
> I will love thee:
> And that love may never cease,
> I will move thee.

('Praise II')

The same masterly simplicity is visible in:

> Throw away thy rod,
> Throw away thy wrath;
> O my God,
> Take the gentle path.

('Discipline')

I wish to end by giving in full the poem which, significantly, I think ends *The Temple*. It is named 'Love III', and indicates the serenity finally attained by this proud and humble man:

Love bade me welcome: yet my soul drew back,
    Guiltie of dust and sinne.
But quick-ey'd Love, observing me grow slack
    From my first entrance in,
Drew nearer to me, sweetly questioning,
    If I lack'd any thing.

A guest, I answer'd, worthy to be here:
    Love said, You shall be he.
I the unkinde, ungratefull? Ah my deare,
    I cannot look on thee.
Love took my hand, and smiling did reply,
    Who made the eyes but I?

Truth Lord, but I have marr'd them: let my shame
    Go where it doth deserve.
And know you not, sayes Love, who bore the blame?
    My deare, then I will serve.
You must sit down, sayes Love, and taste my meat:
    So I did sit and eat.

Notes

1. Four editions of *The Temple* appeared within three years of its first publication; its popularity continued to the end of the century. In the eighteenth century Herbert's poems were generally disparaged: Cowper, for instance, though he found in them a strain of piety which he admired, regarded them as 'gothick and uncouth', and this was the universal opinion of that age. The restoration of Herbert's reputation was begun by Coleridge who, in a letter to William Collins, dated 6th December 1818, writes: '... I find more substantial comfort now in pious George Herbert's "Temple" which I used to read to amuse myself with his quaintness – in short, only to laugh at – than in all the poetry since the poems of Milton. If you have not read Herbert, I can recommend the book to you confidently. The poem entitled "The Flower" is especially affecting; and, to me, such a phrase as "and relish versing" expresses a sincerity, a reality, which I would unwillingly exchange for the more dignified "and once more love the Muse" &c. And so, with many other of Herbert's homely phrases.' (*Letters*, vol IV, edited by Earl Leslie Griggs, 1959).

   Writing to Lady Beaumont in 1826, Coleridge says: 'My dear old friend Charles Lamb and I differ widely (and in point of taste and moral feeling this is a rare occurrence) in our estimate and liking of George Herbert's sacred poems. He greatly prefers Quarles – nay he dislikes Herbert.' (*The Letters of Charles Lamb*, edited by E. V. Lucas, vol. I, 1935).

2. By Mario Praz, whose *Seicentismo e marinismo in Inghilterra* is essential for the study of Crashaw in particular.

3. A. Alvarez in *The School of Donne* says justly of this stanza: 'This is, I suppose, the most perfect and most vivid stanza in the whole of Herbert's work. But it is, in every sense, so natural that its originality is easily missed.' (See also Coleridge on this poem: footnote to p. 1 above.)

Select Bibliography

BIBLIOGRAPHIES

A Herbert Bibliography, by G. H. Palmer (Cambridge, Mass: Library of Harvard University Bibliographical Contributions, 1911). A privately printed catalogue for the compiler's collection of books by and about Herbert. Useful but incomplete.

A Bibliography of Studies in Metaphysical Poetry, 1939–1960, compiled by L. E. Berry (Madison: University of Wisconsin Press, 1964).

Four Metaphysical Poets: George Herbert, Richard Crashaw, Henry Vaughan, Andrew Marvell. A bibliographical catalogue of the early editions of their poetry and prose to the end of the seventeenth century, by Anthony F. Allison (Folkestone and London: Dawsons, 1973).

WORKS BY GEORGE HERBERT

Collected works

The Works, with Preface by W. Pickering and Notes by S. T. Coleridge, 2 vols (London, 1835–6).

The Complete Works, ed. A. B. Grosart, 3 vols (London, 1874). Textually most unreliable, but the first edition to make use of the Williams MS.

The English Works Newly Arranged, ed. G. H. Palmer, 3 vols (London: Hodder & Stoughton, 1905–7). An important edition, notwithstanding some editorial liberties and speculations.

The Works of George Herbert, ed. F. E. Hutchinson (Oxford: Clarendon, 1941). The definitive edition in the Oxford English Texts Series. The World's Classics reprint (1961) has a valuable introduction by Helen Gardner.

The Complete English Poems: George Herbert, ed. John Tobin (London: Penguin Books, 1991).

Selections

Selected Poems of George Herbert, ed. Douglas Brown (London: Hutchinson Educational, 1960).

The Latin Poetry of George Herbert: A Bilingual Edition, translated by M. M. McCloskey and P. R. Murphy (Athens, Ohio: Ohio University Press, 1965).

Select Hymns Taken Out of Mr Herbert's Temple (1697), with an introduction by W. E. Stephenson (Los Angeles: William Andrews Clark Memorial Library, University of California, 1962).

A Choice of George Herbert's Verse, selected with an introduction by R. S. Thomas (London: Faber, 1967).

Selected Poems of George Herbert, ed. with an introduction, commentary and notes by Gareth Reeves (London: Heinemann, 1971).

George Herbert, selected by W. H. Auden (Harmondsworth: Penguin, 1973).

The English Poems of George Herbert, ed. C. A. Patrides (London: Dent, 1974).

Separate works

The Temple, Sacred Poems and Private Ejaculations (Cambridge, 1633). Thirteen editions were published before 1709 but none thereafter until 1799. The Nonesuch Press edition 1927) ed. F. Meynell (with a bibliographical note by G. Keynes) is based on the Bodleian MS (Tanner 307) which was the copy licensed in 1633 for the printer by the Cambridge Vice-Chancellor and his assessors. Reprinted Menston, England (1968).

Witts Recreations. With a Thousand Outlandish Proverbs Selected by Mr G. H. (London, 1640). The proverbs attributed to Herbert were published separately in 1651 as *Jacula Prudentum.*

Herbert's Remains (London, 1652). Contains most of *A Priest to the Temple* and *Jacula Prudentum.*

A Priest to the Temple, Or, The Country Parson His Character, and Rule of Holy Life (London, 1671). A selection, ed. G. M. Forbes, was published in 1949.

Herbert contributed Latin and Greek poems to the following memorial collections: *Epicedium Cantabrigiense, in Obitum Henrici Principis Walliae* (Cambridge, 1612), 2 Latin poems; *Lacrymae Cantabrigienses, in Obitum Reginae Annae* (Cambridge, 1619), 1 Latin poem; *True Copies of the Latinae Orations, made at Cambridge on the 25 and 27 of Februarie last past* (London, 1623), 1 Latin oration with English translation; *Oratio qua Principis Caroli Reditum ex Hispaniis Celebravit Georgius Herbert* (Cambridge, 1623), 1 Latin oration; *Memoriae Francisi, Baronis de*

Verulamio, Sacrum (London, 1626), 1 Latin poem; *A Sermon of Commemorations of the Lady Danvers by John Donne. Together with other Commemorations of her, called Parentalia by her Sonne, G. Herbert* (London, 1627), 19 Latin and Greek poems.

The Williams MS of George Herbert's Poems: A Facsimile Reproduction with an Introduction by Amy M. Charles (Demlar, NY: Scholars' Facsimiles and Reprints, 1977).

The Bodleian Manuscript of George Herbert's Poems: A Facsimile of Tanner 307, introductions by Amy M. Charles and Mario A. Di Cesare (Delmar, NY: Scholars' Facsimiles and Reprints, 1984).

The Country Parson; The Temple, edited with an introduction by John N. Wall (London: SPCK, 1981).

BIOGRAPHICAL AND CRITICAL STUDIES

Alvarez, Alfred, *The School of Donne* (London: Chatto & Windus, 1961).

Asals, Heather A. R., *Equivocal Prediction: George Herbert's Way to God* (Toronto: University of Toronto Press, 1981).

Benet, Diana, *Secretary of Praise. The Poetic Vocation of George Herbert* (Columbia: University of Missouri Press, 1984).

Bennett, Joan, *Four Metaphysical Poets* (Cambridge: Cambridge University Press, 1934; revised, 1953). Reissued, 1959, with new section on Herbert, as *Five Metaphysical Poets*, and reprinted (1964).

Bloch, Chana, *Spelling the Word. George Herbert and the Bible* (Berkeley: University of California Press, 1985).

Bottrall, Margaret, *George Herbert* (London: Murray, 1954).

Burns, Robert Shaw, *The Call of God: The Theme of Vocation in the Poetry of Donne and Herbert* (Cambridge, Mass: Harvard University Press, 1981).

Charles, Amy M., *A Life of George Herbert* (Ithaca: Cornell University Press, 1977).

Chute, Marchette, *Two Gentle Men* (American edition, 1959; London: Secker & Warburg, 1960). Biographies of Herbert and Herrick.

Clements, Arthur L., *Poetry of Contemplation: John Donne, George Herbert, Henry Vaughan and the Modern Period* (Albany: State University of New York Press, 1990).

Coleridge, Samuel Taylor, *Biographia Literaria* (London, 1817). Chapters xix and xx.

Di Cesare, Mario A., and Rigo Mignani (eds), *A Concordance to the Complete Writings of George Herbert* (Ithaca: Cornell University Press, 1977).

Edgecombe, Rodney, *'Sweetnesse Readie Penn'd: Imagery, Syntax and Metrics in the Poetry of George Herbert* (Salzburg: Institut für Anglistik und Amerikanistik, Universität Salzburg, 1980).

Empson, William, *Seven Types of Ambiguity* (London, 1930).

Fish, Stanley Eugene, *Self-Consuming Artifacts: The Experience of Seventeenth Century Literature* (Berkeley: University of California Press, 1972).

Fish, Stanley Eugene, *The Living Temple: George Herbert and Catechizing* (Berkeley: University of California Press, 1978).

Freer, Colburn, *Music for a King: George Herbert's Style and the Metrical Psalms* (Baltimore: Johns Hopkins University Press, 1972).

Grierson, Herbert, J. C., (ed.), *Metaphysical Poems and Lyrics of the Seventeenth Century*, with an introduction by H. Grierson (Oxford: Clarendon, 1921; reprint, Oxford University Press, 1959).

Harman, Barbara Leah, *Costly Monuments: Representations of the Self in George Herbert's Poetry* (Cambridge, Mass: Harvard University Press, 1982).

Heaney, Seamus, *The Redress of Poetry*, 'An inaugural lecture delivered before the University of Oxford on 24th October 1989' (Oxford: Clarendon, 1990). The publication pays particular attention to George Herbert.

Higgins, Dick, *George Herbert's Pattern Poems in their Tradition* (West Glover, Vt: Unpublished Editions, 1977).

Knights, Lionel, C.., *Exploration: Essays in Criticism Mainly on the Literature of the Seventeenth Century* (London: Chatto & Windus, 1946; reprinted 1976). Contains his essay on Herbert first printed in *Scrutiny*, 1933.

Leishman, James B., *The Metaphysical Poets* (Oxford: The Clarendon Press, 1934).

Lewalski, Barbara Keifer, *Protestant Poetics and the Seventeenth-Century Religious Lyric* (Princeton: Princeton University Press, 1979).

Lull, Janis, *The Poem in Time: Reading George Herbert's Revisions of 'The Church'* (Newark: University of Delaware Press, 1990).

Mann, Cameron, *A Concordance to the English Poems* (Boston and New York: Houghton Mifflin Co, 1927).

Martz, Louis L. (ed.), *George Herbert and Henry Vaughan* (Oxford: Oxford University Press, 1986).

Miller, Edmund, *Drudgerie Divine: The Rhetoric of God and Man in George Herbert* (Salzburg: Institut für Anglistik und Amerikanistik, Universität Salzburg, 1979).

Miller, Edmund, and Di Yanni, Robert (eds), *Like Season'd Timber: New Essays on George Herbert* (New York: Lang, 1987).

Pahlka, William, H., *Saint Augustine's Meter and George Herbert's Will* (Kent, Ohio and London: Kent State University Press, 1988).

Patrick, John Max, and Alan Roper, *The Editor as Critic and the Critic as Editor: Papers Read at a Clark Library Seminar, November 13, 1971*, with an introduction by Murray Kreiger (Los Angeles: William Andrews Clark Memorial Library, University of California, 1973).

Patrides, C. A. (ed.), *George Herbert: The Critical Heritage* (London: Routledge & Kegan Paul, 1983).

Praz, Mario, *Seicentismo e Marinismo in Inghilterra* (Florence: La Voce, 1925).

Praz, Mario, *Studies in Seventeenth Century Imagery* (Rome: Edizioni di Storia e Letteratura; London: Studies of the Warburg Institute, 1939); revised and enlarged edition, 1964.

Ray, Roberr H. (ed.), *The Herbert Allusion Book: Allusions to George Herbert in the Seventeenth Century* (Chapel Hill, NC: University of North Carolina Press, 1986).

Rickey, Mary Ellen, *Utmost Art: Complexity in the Verse of George Herbert* (Lexington, Ky: University of Kentucky Press, 1966).

Roberts, John R., *George Herbert: An Annotated Bibliography of Modern Criticism, 1905–1984* (Columbia: University of Missouri Press, 1978; revised edition 1988).

Roberts, John R., (ed.), *Essential Articles for the Study of George Herbert's Poetry* (Hamden, Conn: Archon Books, 1979).

Schoenfeldt, Michael C., *Prayer and Power: George Herbert and Renaissance Courtship* (Chicago: University of Chicago Press, 1991).

Seelig, Sharon Cadman, *The Shadow of Eternity: Belief and Structure in Herbert, Vaughan and Traherne* (Lexington, Ky: University of Kentucky Press, 1981).

Singleton, Marion White, *God's Courtier: Configuring a Different Grace in George Herbert's Temple* (Cambridge: Cambridge University Press, 1987).

Stein, Arnold, *George Herbert's Lyrics* (Baltimore: John Hopkins University Press, 1968).

Stewart, Stanley, *George Herbert* (Boston, Mass: Twayne Publishers, 1986).

Strier, Richard, *Love Known: Theology and Experience in George Herbert's Poetry* (Chicago, University of Chicago Press, 1983).

Summers, Claude J., and Pebworth, Ted-Larry (eds), *'Too Rich to Clothe the Sunne': Essays on George Herbert* (Pittsburg, Pa: University of Pittsburg Press, 1980).

Summers, Joseph H., *George Herbert: His Religion and Art* (London: Chatto & Windus, 1954; reprinted Binghampton: Center for Medieval and Early Renaissance Studies, 1981).

Swardson, Harold, R., *Poetry and the Fountain of Light: Observations on the conflict between Christian and classical traditions in seventeenth century poetry* (London: Allen & Unwin, 1962).

Taylor, Mark, *The Soul in Paraphrase: George Herbert's Poetics* (The Hague & Paris: Mouton, 1974).

Thorpe, Douglas, *A New Earth: The Labor of Language in Pearl, Herbert's Temple, and Blake's Jerusalem* (Washington, DC: Catholic University of America Press, 1991).

Todd, Richard, *The Opacity of Signs: Acts of Interpretation in George Herbert's The Temple* (Columbia: University of Missouri Press, 1986).

Tuve, Rosamund, *A Reading of George Herbert* (London: Faber, 1952; revised edition, 1965).

Veith, Gene Edward Jr., *Reformation Spirituality, The Religion of George Herbert* (Lewisburg, Pa: Bucknell University Press, 1985).

Vendler, Helen, *The Poetry of George Herbert* (Cambridge, Mass: Harvard University Press, 1975).

Walpole, H. (ed.), *The Life of Lord Herbert of Cherbury* (London, 1764). See also Lord Herbert's *Poems*, ed. Moore Smith (Oxford, 1923).

Walton, Isaac, *The Life of Mr George Herbert* (London, 1670). Reprinted in Walton's *Lives* (1670: World's Classics edition, 1923; with a preface by Patrick Magee, Salisbury: Perdix, 1988).

Westerweel, Bart, *Patterns and Patterning: A Study of Four Poems by George Herbert* (Amsterdam: Rodopi, 1984).

Williamson, George, *The Donne Tradition* (Cambridge, Mass: Harvard University Press, 1930; reprinted, New York, Noonday Press, 1958.

George Herbert Journal, vol. 1–, Fall, 1977–, Bridgeport, Conn. (1977–).

Index

Andrewes, Bishop Lancelot, 16, 17
Anglicanism, 2, 3, 6, 16
Arnold, Matthew, 6
Auden, W. H., 3, 4

Bach, J. S., 6
Bacon, Sir Francis, 16
baroque, 6
Bellarmine, Cardinal, 28
Bemerton, Wiltshire, 18, 25
Benlowes, Edward, 26
Bhagavad Gītā , 29
Burnet, Bishop, 3

Calvinists, 17
Carnarvon, Earl of, 13
Church Fathers, 19
Church of England, 3, 16–21, 27, 32
Cleveland, John, 26
Coleridge, S. T., 2
Cook, Sir Robert, 17–18
Court, 17, 27
Cowley, Abraham, 26
Crashaw, Richard, 22, 25, 26, 32

Dante, 3
Danvers, Jane, 17

Danvers, Lord, 17
Danvers, Sir John, 16
'Divine discontent', 9
Donne, John, 1, 2, 4, 5, 6, 7, 14, 15, 17, 22–6, 32–7,
   'The Autumnal', 15
   'Batter my heart ...', 5, 23–5
   Holy Sonnets, 5, 7
   'Nocturnall upon S. Lucies Day', 37
   'Since she whom I loved ...', 5
   'The Sunne Rising', 36

Eliot, T. S., 2, 3–4, 10
   For Lancelot Andrewes, 2
   Thoughts After Lambeth, 2
Empson, William, 4
   Seven Types of Ambiguity, 27–8

Ferrar, Nicholas (of Little Gidding), 6, 17, 25

Gardner, Helen, 21
Gongora, Luis de, 26
Grierson, Herbert J. C., 22, 23

Henry VII, 13
Herbert, Edward (Lord

Herbert of Cherbury),
    7, 14, 15
Herbert, George
    'Affliction I', 29
    'Affliction IV', 35
    'The Altar', 36
    'The Answer', 7
    'The British Church', 3
    'The Church Floore', 34
    'Church-monuments', 34
    'The Collar', 19–20
    'Deniall', 35, 38
    'Dialogue-Anthem of the
        Christian and Death',
        7–8
    'The Discharge', 35
    'Discipline', 9, 38
    'Easter', 37
    'Easter Wings', 4, 36
    'Faith', 34
    'The Flower', 30–1
    'Good Friday', 36, 37
    'Holy Baptisme I', 37
    'Jordan I', 5
    'Love III', 38–9
    'Mattens', 34
    'Miserie', 38
    'Mortification', 35
    'Obedience', 32–3
    'Praise I', 8–9
    'Praise II', 38
    'Prayer I', 4, 5, 23–5
    A Priest in the Temple, Or,
        The Country Parson His
        Character etc, 18–19
    'The Quiddity', 10
    'The Quip', 33
    'Redemption', 34
    'Repentance', 37
    'The Sacrifice', 27–8, 36
    'Sepulchre', 36
    'Sighs and Grones', 37
    'The Temper I', 29–30

The Temple, 6, 17, 22–31
    'The Trellis', 4
    'Ungratefulnesse', 35
    'Vanitie', 35
    'Whitsunday', 30
    'The Windows', 9-10, 35
    World's Classics ed. 1907
        introduction, quoted,
        20–21
    World's Classics 1961
        reprint, 21
Herbert, Lady Magdalen, 4,
    14, 15, 17, 26
Herbert, Richard (Sir Richard
    Herbert of
    Montgomery), 13, 14
Herrick, Robert, 22
Homer, 4
Hopkins, Gerard Manley, 25
Hutchinson, F. E., 21, 25, 27
    quoted, 32

James I, 17
Jeremiah, Lamentations of, 28
Johnson, Samuel, 26
Jonson, Ben, 14

King, Bishop, 22
Knights, L. C., quoted, 25–6,
    27, 33

Marino, Giamabattista, 26
Mass of the Presanctified, 28
Melville, Andrew, 1, 17, 26
metaphysical poets, 2, 7, 23
Montgomery Castle, see
    Herbert, Richard

New Testament, 28
Newport, Sir Richard, 14

Oxford Book of English Verse,
    22

Pascal, Blaise, 7
Pembroke, Earl of, 13
Pope, Alexander, 1, 3
Puritans, 17

Quiller-Couch, Sir Arthur, 22

Rimbaud, Arthur, 3
Romantics, 2

Scholastics, 19, 28
'the school of Donne', 2, 7,
    22–3, 25, 26, 32
Shakespeare, William
    Hamlet, 9
    Sonnet 66, 4

Thirty-Nine Articles, the, 3
Traherne, Thomas, 26
Trinity College, Cambridge,
    15, 16
Tuve, Rosamund
    A Reading of George
    Herbert, 28

Vaughan, Henry, 26, 32

Wales, 13
Walton, Isaac
    Life, 2
    quoted, 6, 16, 17, 18
Wars of the Roses, the, 13
Westminster School, 16
wit, 24, 33

*Recent and
Forthcoming Titles
in the
New Series of*

WRITERS AND
THEIR WORK

WRITERS AND THEIR WORK

RECENT & FORTHCOMING TITLES

Title	Author
Angela Carter	*Lorna Sage*
John Clare	*John Lucas*
Joseph Conrad	*Cedric Watts*
John Donne	*Stevie Davies*
William Hazlitt	*J.B. Priestley; R.L. Brett (introduction by Michael Foot)*
Elizabeth Gaskell	*Kate Flint*
William Golding	*Kevin McCarron*
King Lear	*Terence Hawkes*
Doris Lessing	*Elizabeth Maslen*
Children's Literature	*Kimberley Reynolds*
Ian McEwan	*Kiernan Ryan*
Christopher Marlowe	*Thomas Healy*
Andrew Marvell	*Annabel Patterson*
Walter Pater	*Laurel Brake*
Dorothy Richardson	*Carol Watts*
The Sensation Novel	*Lyn Pykett*

TITLES IN PREPARATION

Title	Author
W.H. Auden	*Stan Smith*
Aphra Behn	*Sue Wiseman*
Jane Austen	*Robert Clark*
Geoffrey Chaucer	*Steve Ellis*
Henry Fielding	*Jenny Uglow*
Graham Greene	*Peter Mudford*
Hamlet	*Ann Thompson & Neil Taylor*
David Hare	*Jeremy Ridgman*
Thomas Hardy	*Peter Widdowson*
Henry James - The Later Novels	*Barbara Hardy*
James Joyce	*Steve Connor*
D.H. Lawrence	*Linda Williams*
David Lodge	*Bernard Bergonzi*
Sir Thomas Malory	*Catherine La Farge*
Jean Rhys	*Helen Carr*
Edmund Spencer	*Colin Burrow*
J.R.R. Tolkien	*Charles Moseley*
Mary Wollstonecraft	*Jane Moore*
Virginia Woolf	*Laura Marcus*
William Wordsworth	*Jonathan Bate*

RECENT & FORTHCOMING TITLES

DORIS LESSING
Elizabeth Maslen

Covering a wide range of Doris Lessing's works up to 1992, including all her novels and a selection of her short stories and non-fictional writing, this study demonstrates how Lessing's commitment to political and cultural issues and her explorations of inner space have remained unchanged throughout her career. Maslen also examines Lessing's writings in the context of the work of Bakhtin and Foucault, and of feminist theories.

Elizabeth Maslen is Senior Lecturer in English at Queen Mary and Westfield College, University of London.

0 7463 0705 5 paperback 80pp

JOSEPH CONRAD
Cedric Watts

This authoritative introduction to the range of Conrad's work draws out the distinctive thematic preoccupations and technical devices running through the main phases of the novelist's literary career. Watts explores Conrad's importance and influence as a moral, social and political commentator on his times and addresses recent controversial developments in the evaluation of this magisterial, vivid, complex and problematic author.

Cedric Watts, Professor of English at the University of Sussex, is recognized internationally as a leading authority on the life and works of Joseph Conrad.

0 7463 0737 3 paperback 80pp

JOHN DONNE
Stevie Davies

Raising a feminist challenge to the body of male criticism which congratulates Donne on the 'virility' of his writing, Dr Davies' stimulating and accessible introduction to the full range of the poet's work sets it in the wider cultural, religious and political context conditioning the mind of this turbulent and brilliant poet. Davies also explores the profound emotionalism of Donne's verse and offers close, sensitive readings of individual poems.

Stevie Davies is a literary critic and novelist who has written on a wide range of literature.

0 7463 0738 1 paperback 96pp

JOHN CLARE
John Lucas

Setting out to recover Clare – whose work was demeaned and damaged by the forces of the literary establishment – as a great poet, John Lucas offers the reader the chance to see the life and work of John Clare, the 'peasant poet' from a new angle. His unique and detailed study portrays a knowing, articulate and radical poet and thinker writing as much out of a tradition of song as of poetry. This is a comprehensive and detailed account of the man and the artist which conveys a strong sense of the writer's social and historical context.

John Lucas has written many books on nineteenth- and twentieth-century literature, and is himself a talented poet. He is Professor of English at Loughborough University.

0 7463 0729 2 paperback 96pp

ANGELA CARTER
Lorna Sage

Angela Carter was probable the most inventive British novelist of her generation. In this fascinating study, Lorna Sage argues that one of the reasons for Carter's enormous success is the extraordinary intelligence with which she read the cultural signs of our times – from structuralism and the study of folk tales in the 1960s – to, more recently, fairy stories and gender politics. The book explores the roots of Carter's originality and covers all her novels, as well as some short stories and non-fiction.

Lorna Sage teaches at the University of East Anglia, where she is currently Dean of the School of English and American Studies.

0 7463 0727 6 paperback 96pp

CHILDREN'S LITERATURE
Kimberley Reynolds

Children's literature has changed dramatically in the last hundred years and this book identifies and analyses the dominant genres which have evolved during this period. Drawing on a wide range of critical and cultural theories, Kimberley Reynolds looks at children's private reading, examines the relationship between the child reader and the adult writer, and draws some interesting conclusions about children's literature as a forum for shaping the next generation and as a safe place for developing writers' private fantasies.

Kimberley Reynolds lectures in English and Women's Studies at Roehampton Institute, where she also runs the Children's Literature Research Unit.

0 7463 0728 4 paperback 112pp

THE SENSATION NOVEL
Lyn Pykett

A 'great fact' in the literature of its day, a 'disagreeable' sign of the times, or an ephemeral minor sub-genre? What was the sensation novel, and why did it briefly dominate the literary scene in the 1860s? This wide-ranging study analyses the broader significance of the sensation novel as well as looking at it in its specific cultural context.

Lyn Pykett is Senior Lecturer in English at the University of Wales in Aberystwyth.

0 7463 0725 X paperback 96pp

CHRISTOPHER MARLOWE
Thomas Healy

The first study for many years to explore the whole range of Marlowe's writing, this book uses recent ideas about the relation between literature and history, popular and élite culture, and the nature of Elizabethan theatre to reassess his significance. An ideal introduction to one of the most exciting and innovative of English writers, Thomas Healy's book provides fresh insights into all of Marlowe's important works.

Thomas Healy is Senior Lecturer in English at Birkbeck College, University of London.

0 7463 0707 1 paperback 96pp

ANDREW MARVELL
Annabel Patterson

This state-of-the art guide to one of the seventeenth century's most intriguing poets examines Marvell's complex personality and beliefs and provides a compelling new perspective on his work. Annabel Patterson – one of the leading Marvell scholars – provides comprehensive introductions to Marvell's different self-representations and places his most famous poems in their original context.

Annabel Patterson is Professor of English at Yale University and author of *Marvell and the Civic Crown* (1978).

0 7463 0715 2 paperback 96pp

IAN McEWAN
Kiernan Ryan

This is the first book-length study of one of the most original and exciting writers to have emerged in Britain in recent years. It provides an introduction to the whole range of McEwan's work, examining his novels, short stories and screenplays in depth and tracing his development from the 'succès de scandale' of *First Love, Last Rites* to the haunting vision of the acclaimed *Black Dogs*.

Kiernan Ryan is Fellow and Director of Studies in English at New Hall, University of Cambridge.

0 7463 0742 X paperback 80pp £6.99

ELIZABETH GASKELL
Kate Flint

Recent critical appraisal has focused on Gaskell both as a novelist of industrial England and on her awareness of the position of women and the problems of the woman writer. Kate Flint reveals how for Gaskell the condition of women was inseparable from broader issues of social change. She shows how recent modes of feminist criticism and theories of narrative work together to illuminate the radicalism and experimentalism which we find in Gaskell's fiction.

Kate Flint is University Lecturer in Victorian and Modern English Literature, and Fellow of Linacre College, Oxford.

0 7463 0718 7 paperback 96pp

KING LEAR
Terence Hawkes

In his concise but thorough analysis of *King Lear* Terence Hawkes offers a full and clear exposition of its complex narrative and thematic structure. By examining the play's central preoccupations and through close analysis of the texture of its verse he seeks to locate it firmly in its own history and the social context to which, clearly, it aims to speak. The result is a challenging critical work which both deepens understanding of this great play and illuminates recent approaches to it.

Terence Hawkes has written several books on both Shakespeare and modern critical theory. he is Professor of English at the University of Wales, Cardiff.

0 7463 0739 X paperback 96pp